To
Parker-
With Love .
Christina B. Pope
+

Thomas Berkwill

123 CHARLOTTE

Written by Christina Berkau Pope
Illustrated by Thomas Berkau

CRICKET
VISION
PRESS

Fly with me through the Piedmont land.
New adventures are close at hand.
Charlotte's got a lot to see;
Let's get busy, 1,2,3!

1 One roller coaster climbing high.
Reaching clouds in the Charlotte sky.
Dipping, whirling, screeching round;
Laughter fills the air with sound!

2 Two cyclists traveling with ease.
Cruising down the loop, lined with trees.
Humming, whizzing, on a roll;
Steady pace to reach their goal!

3 Three kayaks skim through waves and rock
Chilly splashes bring grins of shock.
Flowing, bumping to and fro;
Underneath the sun aglow!

4 Four fine canines sitting up tall.
Waiting to pounce and catch the ball.
Wagging, panting side by side;
Loving owners watch with pride!

5 Five musicians begin to play.
Songs performed in clever array.
Tambourines tap to the beat;
Clapping hands and dancing feet!

6 Six skyscrapers bold in design.
Create a vast, regal skyline.
Rising, shining, strong and tall;
Spring, summer, winter & fall!

7
Seven butterflies taking flight.
Swirling through gardens pruned just right.
Batting colored wings with flair;
Floating through the fragrant air!

8 Eight fair geese basking in the sun.
Following the lead, one by one.
Swimming, swirling, gliding by;
Squawking as they start to fly!

9 Nine crates abundant with produce.
Healthy to cook or blend for juice.
Crunching, tasting as a snack;
Farm to fork, a growing knack!

10

Ten objects orbiting in space.
Rotating in a solar race.
Watch the universe expand;
Glowing, tilting, truly grand!

We've traveled through the city wide,
And seen surrounding countryside.
A choice Southern place to stop;
Charlotte ranks right at the top!

123 Charlotte Inspiration

Number 1 is inspired by Carowinds amusement and waterpark. Found on the NC/SC border of I-77, the park is known as the premier entertainment destination of the Carolinas. Planet Snoopy and Boomerang Bay provide the perfect summer escape for your little ones, while taller visitors looking for a thrill will love the new Fury 325. Open for the 2015 season, Fury 325 is the world's tallest and fastest giga coaster with speeds up to 95 mph!

Number 2 pays homage to the popular "Booty Loop" located in the heart of Myers Park, close to Queens University of Charlotte. The 2.8 mile scenic loop, crowned by an arching canopy of tall trees, is a hot spot for local cyclists. The loop is also home to the annual fundraiser, 24 Hours of Booty. Since 2002, this 24 hour cycling event has raised over 14 million dollars for both local and national cancer fighting programs.

Number 3 is in reference to the Catawba River. Stretching 220 miles from the mountains of North Carolina down into South Carolina, the river feeds many reservoirs including Lake Norman and Lake Wylie, both popular destinations for recreation and real estate. The Catawba is also the source for the 700 acre U.S. National Whitewater Center, established in 2006, where rafting and kayaking are two of many outdoor options for fun.

Number 4 is for all of the dog lovers we know…the ones who treat their pups to blueberry facials or organic antler chews on the regular! Charlotte offers an array of activities for those who hate to leave their canines at home. From dog bars and bakeries to festivals and parks designated just for 4 legged breeds, the options are plentiful. Barkingham Park, Swaney Pointe K-9 Park or Davie Dog Park are just a few on the list.

Number 5 is a nod to the Charlotte music scene. Of course Charlotte has large amphitheater and arena shows, drawing huge crowds and international talent, but the modest locales aren't too shabby either. Step off the beaten path to experience more intimate performances. We have several favorites on our roster, including Neighborhood Theatre, Snug Harbor, Tremont Music Hall, The Visulite or The Milestone Club.

Number 6 represents the iconic image true Charlotte natives think of when "coming home". There is something exciting about those tall buildings rising up into view as the interstate winds closer to the city. Charlotte's skyline houses the tallest building in North Carolina, and defines our city as a major United States financial center. Catching a glimpse of an uptown sunset over the Queen City skyscrapers never seems to get old.

Number 7 depicts Daniel Stowe Botanical Garden in the town of Belmont. Just 15 miles west of Charlotte, the garden rests on 400 acres and was created to preserve the region's natural beauty. Children will love Lost Hollow, the magical garden with a sunken pond, aviary and moon keep, while any visitor will enjoy exploring the other hidden sanctuaries, including the 8,000 square foot Orchid Conservatory (my favorite)!

Number 8 is dedicated to my son who finds great joy in visiting our native geese population. Though Canadian Geese are often considered pesky by local parks and recreation officials, they can be a lifesaver for moms of toddlers looking for free entertainment! Popular destinations for these wildlife creatures include Park Road Park, Freedom Park, Marshall Park, McAlpine Creek Park, and any lakefront venues or subdivisions with water.

Number 9 recognizes the growing trend towards sustainable, community based dining. Increasingly, Charlotte restaurant owners and farmers are teaming up to provide fresh, local and delicious options. Daily and weekly menu changes reflect the seasonal goodness of the South! But rest assured, farm to fork is happening at home as well. With neighborhood markets popping up all over the city, stocking up on healthy, organic choices has never been easier.

Number 10 is inspired by the Schiele Museum of Natural History. Located in Gastonia, a satellite city of the Charlotte metropolitan area, the Schiele houses the James H. Lynn Planetarium. Visitors experience a life-like representation of our solar system using images from the Hubble Telescope and other space expeditions. In addition to stargazing, museum patrons can adventure through wildlife habitats, American Indian culture or 18th Century farmland.

For our grandmother, Moetta. The sharpest 95 year old we know and a true beauty
both inside and out. She loves the Lord & her family, still makes a mean deer
sandwich, and can outsmart us any day of the week at Rook or Bridge. We are
grateful for your influence, Grandma.

123 Charlotte

Text copyright 2015 by Christina Berkau Pope
Illustrations copyright 2015 by Thomas Berkau
First Edition 2015

Graphic Design Services by Pete Hurdle

Cricket Vision Press
1116 Linda Lane
Charlotte, North Carolina 28211
www.cricketvisionpress.com

ISBN: 978-0-9963679-0-5

Display and text type set in Clarendon and Square Meal
Each illustration is hand drawn prior to adding full digital color
Printed in Korea by Pacom